Library of Congress Cataloging in Publication Data
Yabuuchi, Masayuki, 1940-
Animals sleeping.

Translation of: Dō yatte neru no ka na.
Summary: Simple text and pictures show sleeping
habits of the koala, leopard, sea otter, and albatross,
and of flamingos, bats, and camels.
1. Animal behavior – Juvenile literature. 2. Sleep –
Juvenile literature. [1. Animals – Habits and behavior.
2. Sleep] I. Title.
QL751.5.Y313   1983   599.05   82-24620
ISBN 0-399-20983-2

Published in the United States in 1983 by Philomel Books,
a division of The Putnam Publishing Group,
51 Madison Avenue, New York, NY 10010.
Printed in Japan.

Animals Sleeping

Masayuki Yabuuchi

PHILOMEL BOOKS

New York

Do you know how
flamingos sleep?

They sleep standing on one leg.

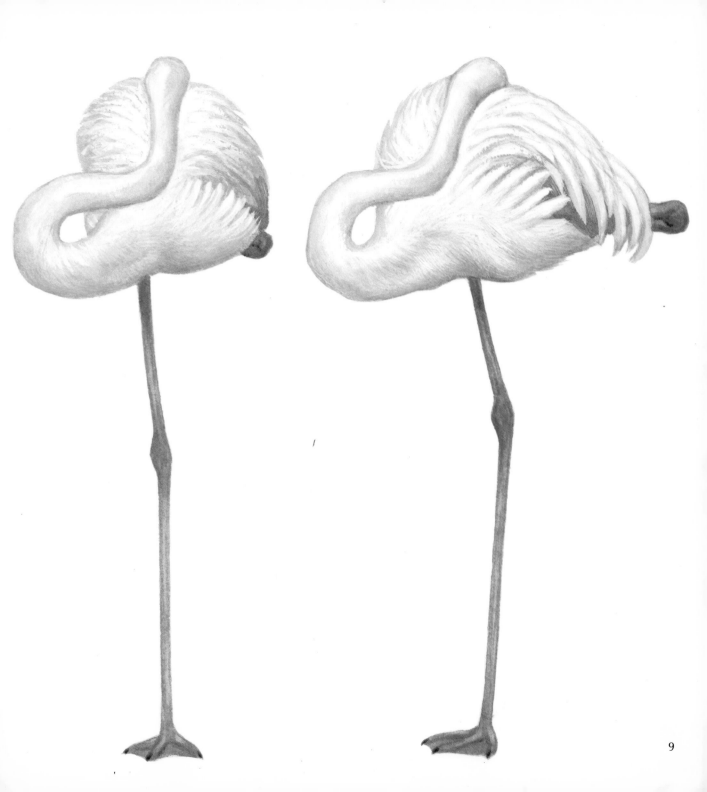

9

How does the leopard sleep?

It sleeps lying
along the
branch of a tree.

How do bats sleep?

They sleep hanging upside down.

The sea otter floats on the water
when it is awake...

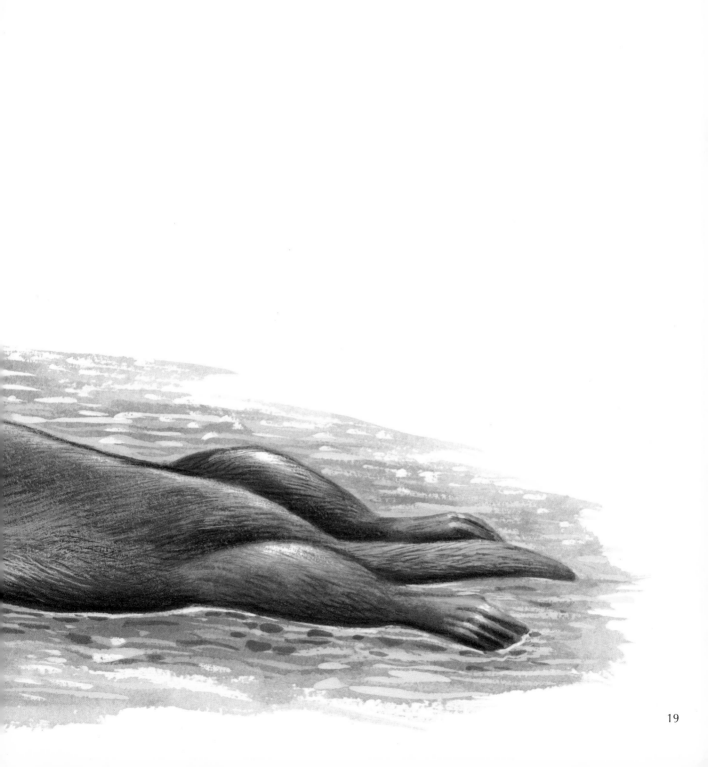

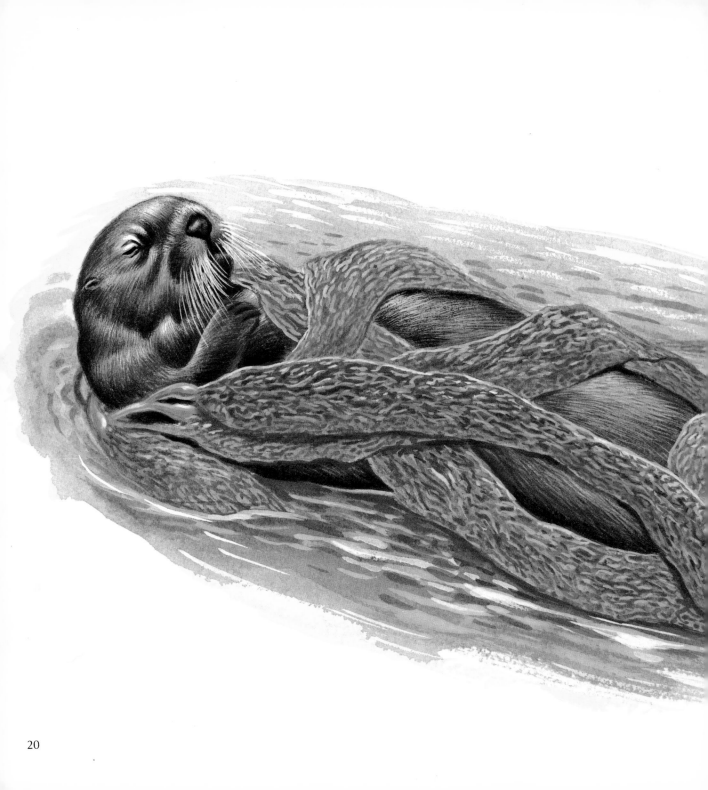

...and when it is asleep.

How does the albatross sleep?

It sleeps floating on the sea.

25

And how do camels sleep?

27

Camels sleep lying on
the ground, with their legs
tucked underneath them.